THE MAN'S MANIFESTO

REDISCOVERING THE MAN WITHIN THE MALE

"A MAN'S GOT TO HAVE A CODE, A CREED TO LIVE BY..."

JOHN WAYNE

CONTENTS

ACKNOWLEDGMENTS

I would just like to acknowledge some of the great men in my life who have inspired me to strive toward becoming a great man.

My father in law, Huey McDonald.

My spiritual father, David Garcia.

My second dad, Bruce Doan.

My mentors, spiritual leaders, and friends: Dr. Michael Brown, Dr. Alan Ehler, Terry Raburn, Scott Young, Bill Wynn, Jim Rodriguez, Ron Dixon, Allen Griffin, Pat Schatzline, Jeff Drapp, Tony Parker, Jaime Perez, and all my RPM brothers.

I dedicate this book to my sons, Ty and Elijah. May you both grow in wisdom and stature as you become the men that God has destined you to be.

WHAT OTHERS ARE SAYING

In an easy read creative style Brent Simpson offers substantive and practical help to dads. I strongly recommend MAN'S MANIFESTO to all fathers who want to help a son reach his potential.

- Bob Rhoden, author FOUR FACES OF A LEADER

Ministering to men for over 25 year I have witnessed the devastation that the lack of role models, extended adolescence, and the feminization of manhood has brought down on men, their marriages, and families. Through his own desire to lead his son to manhood Brent Simpson developed "The Man's Manifesto" a resource that not only gives manhood a definition, but models it through real life examples. I am pleased to recommend this resource to fathers leading their sons to manhood, and men seeking a clearer definition of what it means to be a godly man!

- John Hensel, Men's Director for the Peninsular Florida District Council of the Assemblies of God

Brent Simpson has penned a powerful message to men coming of age to let them know what they will need to do to become great men. This powerfully moving book is filled with real examples of men who have lived out the ten characteristics of great men. It is written in a way that will grab the mind and heart of those stepping out of puberty as well as those well down the road of manhood. Fathers should share this book with their sons and together commit and seek God's help to become the men they were created to be.

- Dr. Alan Ehler, Dean, College of Christian Ministry and Religion, Southeastern University

I am convinced that this is a book that every man should read and also that every boy, especially teenagers, should read and make the powerful truths applicable to their individual journey with the Lord on a daily basis! I highly recommend this book to men, for it is my conviction that if they will take the powerful truths contained in this book and make them a part of their daily lives, they will truly become Men of God!

- W. Gene Petty, former Superintendent of the Northern New England District of the Assemblies of God

A Man's Manifesto" is a priceless handbook of godly principles for raising a son in a counter Christian society. The ten tenets of manhood Brent expounds on are solid biblical guidelines for any mentor wanting to raise protégés with absolute truths. This book will leave a lasting legacy to all who read it, young or old. It will challenge and refine manhood values in older men and show a young man the proper choices he is to make. I plan to use this book for our church ministry to young boys. I enthusiastically recommend "A Man's Manifesto.

- David Garcia,
Lead Pastor, Grace World Outreach Church

Brent Simpson has reverse-engineered victory and placed the reader in a position to win! As a father of two boys and a concerned Christian leader, there are few areas that need our attention more than today's generation of men. Many have fallen on the anvil of parenting analytics instead of addressing the spiritual and natural needs within all men. This book helps us capture the lightning of our Lord's leadership to invest in our men, both young and old. I believe every father should read this book alongside his son.

- Allen Griffin, Evangelist, AG Ministries.

FORWARD

Patrick Schatzline
Evangelist & Author, Remnant Ministries International

I am personally deeply excited about this powerful new book from my friend, Pastor & author Brent Simpson called, "Man's Manifesto." What was originally written as a message of love, encouragement and coaching for his son has now become a mandate for all Father's, Grandfathers and surrogates to instill in the next generation what it truly means to be a man. In this powerful message of truth you will be inspired to lead with character, honor and strength.

You will realize quickly that this is a road map to discover the lost's truths that have been left dormant in a fatherless society. I have seen in the eyes of tens of thousands of young people the wounded spirit caused by the abandonment of a Father. Men we must pick up the baton of leadership in our homes, churches and communities and restore the hearts of this generation. I once heard it said, "Wounded boys create angry fathers."

Now more than ever the concept of "manhood" is under attack from every aspect of society. In fact manhood is actually frowned upon by today's academic elite and cultural police as being out of touch machoism.

They are wrong!

We must teach our sons what it means to be a warrior. I am reminded of when Gideon finally chased down his enemies named Zebah and Zalmunna in Judges chapter 8. Gideon turned to his son Jether and told him to kill the these evil men, but suddenly the son refused out of fear. Then the enemies turned to Gideon and reminded him of this powerful truth when they said in Judges 8:21, "Come, do it yourself. 'As is the man, so is his strength.'" We must not ask the next generation to kill what we would not confront. As men we must make up our minds to raise up the next generation as Godly voices of valor.

We must release to them the power of manhood! This generation is in trouble. We must make up our minds to no longer be echo's of yesterday's failures, but voices of promise to their tomorrow. There is a reason that God the Father ripped open the heavens with his voice and declared, "This is my Son, whom I love; with him I am well pleased. (Matthew 3:17)"

God was letting the world know that his boy made him proud. This is our example! Together we can raise boys into men or we will suffer the consequences of watching boys forever stay children.

This is not just another book to sit on a shelf gathering dust, but rather this book with words, pictures and pulse will be used from generation to generation! This book is a right-now message! Martin Luther once said, "If you want to change the world pick up your pen and write ." That is exactly what Brent Simpson has done! I say to my friend Brent, "*Bravo!*"

INTRODUCTION

I mean to make myself a man, and if I succeed in that, I shall succeed in everything else.

James A. Garfield

Gentlemen,

It is my great honor to participate in your journey from malehood into manhood. We live in a day when manliness and manhood have lost their true virtue. Our world is full of males - But examples of genuine masculinity are few and far between. In fact, most males today cannot even define manhood. And how can a young male grow up to be a great man if he doesn't have a standard of manhood to aspire to? Without strong examples, most young men don't know what a man is supposed to look like, act like and be like. Great men are an endangered species, and fewer young men than ever will have the opportunity to learn from them.

It is for this reason that I write this book. John Wayne once said, "A man's got to have a code, a creed to live by."

This book endeavors to share some of that creed - the DNA of great men. You must understand that there is a standard *Great men are an endangered species* of manhood - and that you are expected to live up to it. As feminized males are celebrated more often, it will become even less often that you see genuine manliness modeled. There may only be a few men worthy of you following their example. Therefore, I have written this book to guide you on the path to genuine manliness.

"We do not admire the man of timid peace. We admire the man who embodies victorious effort; the man who never wrongs his neighbor, who is prompt to help a friend, but who has those virile qualities necessary to win in the stern strife or actual life."

-Theodore Roosevelt

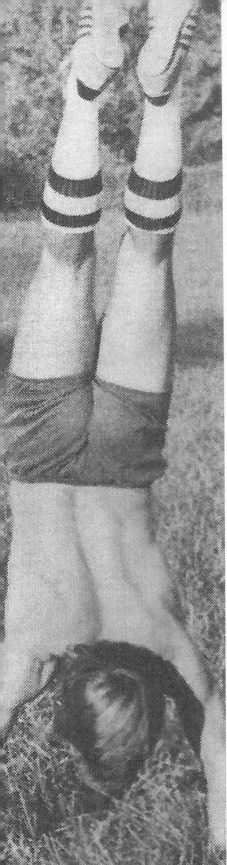

This book may be short, but its expectations are high, and its call is life-changing. To aspire to be a man is to aspire for greatness. It's a life-long quest. You may need to refer to this book throughout your life as it will serve as a *This book may be short, but its expectations are high, and its call is life-changing.* guidepost as you become a husband, a father and even a grandfather. It will teach you how to react during challenging circumstances, how to confront evil with resolve and how to live a life worthy of the high calling of the nobility of genuine manhood.

"The superior man is he who develops, in harmonious proportions, his moral, intellectual and physical nature. This should be the end at which men of all classes should aim, and it is this only which constitutes real greatness"
–Douglas Jerrold

Manliness is far more than the size of your truck tires, biceps, or bank account. In fact, the size of your heart matters far more than the size of your male parts. Great men are not defined by the weight they can lift, the amount they can drink or the women they have had sex with. Manliness is so much more than scaling mountains, killing animals and finishing fights.

Manliness is defined by courage, honor, heart and faith. It's an inner strength that doesn't allow you to compromise your convictions and it holds you together when everyone else is falling apart. Manliness is a beautiful combination of integrity, character, chivalry, and grit. A man will face storms, brave winds and swim upstream. A man is strong enough to fight in wars, gentle enough to cradle his newborn baby, and wise enough to both recognize and control the plethora of emotions that live in between these extremes.

A man is strong enough to fight in wars, gentle enough to cradle his newborn baby, and wise enough to both recognize and control the plethora of emotions that live in between these extremes.

To embrace becoming a man is a noble quest that is undertaken one decision at a time over the course of a lifetime. I believe that God has deposited greatness in you. I pray this little book will help you discover the great man that I believe lies within you.

In the pages of this book you will hear stories, quotes and thoughts on manhood from some of the great men who have come before you. Learn from them. Follow their example. And you too will become a great man.

A man does what he must -- in spite of personal consequences, in spite of obstacles and dangers and pressures and that is the basis of all human morality.

Winston Churchill

"Men cannot be men—much less good or heroic men—unless their actions have meaningful consequences to people they truly care about. Strength requires an opposing force, courage requires risk, mastery requires hard work, honor requires accountability to other men.

Without these things, we are little more than boys playing at being men, and there is no weekend retreat or mantra or half-assed rite of passage that can change that.

A rite of passage must reflect a real change in status and responsibility for it to be anything more than theater. No reimagined manhood of convenience can hold its head high so long as the earth remains the tomb of our ancestors"

Jack Donovan

A MAN HAS GRIT

A man works hard and doesn't quit amidst opposition.

Grit. It's hard to define, but you know it when you see it. It's not talked about very often these days because it's rare. But grit is the single most important contributor that leads toward success. Grit is a combination of courage, hard work, perseverance, passion, resolve and tenacity. It has almost nothing to do with your IQ, personal talents, or ability to learn, but has everything to do with what you accomplish in life. John Wayne and Chuck Norris optimize grit. If it was summed up in one word it would be "tenacity." Grit is seen in a man's work ethic, his resolve, and his ability to keep marching forward when life pushes against him.

Grit is a combination of courage, hard work, perseverance, passion, resolve and tenacity.

President Theodore Roosevelt was a man's man. He led the 1st United States Volunteer Cavalry during the Spanish American War in 1898. They were known as the "Rough Riders" and were some of the toughest men to ever join the military. They were the Navy Seals and Army Rangers of their day! President Roosevelt was a man with grit.

During the presidential campaign of 1912, Theodore Roosevelt was shot in the chest by a would-be assassin while leaving his hotel in Milwaukee. Before lodging in his chest, the bullet passed through Roosevelt's metal eyeglass case and a 50-page speech folded in his breast pocket. Since he did not start coughing up blood, Roosevelt figured the bullet had not penetrated his lung. Without a second thought, he continued on to the auditorium and delivered his speech.

His address began with these words: "Friends, I shall ask you to be as quiet as possible. I don't know whether you fully understand that I have just been shot; but it takes more than that to kill a Bull Moose. ... The bullet is in me now, so that I cannot make a very long speech, but I will try my best." [1]

His speech lasted 90 minutes...

Theodore Roosevelt was a bull moose of a man. He had Grit—an indomitable spirit. A bullet in the chest was a minor setback.

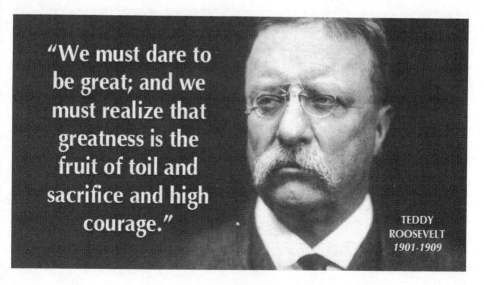

"We must dare to be great; and we must realize that greatness is the fruit of toil and sacrifice and high courage."

TEDDY ROOSEVELT
1901-1909

Grit causes you to keep moving forward when others would quit. Grit doesn't take no for an answer and keeps believing when the first attempt fails.

The Beatles were turned down by the Decca recording company and told that "guitar music is on the way out." Boy were they wrong!

Ulysses S. Grant failed as a soldier, farmer and real estate agent. At age 38 he had to return home to go work for his father as a handy man.... but he kept pressing forward and at age 46, he was elected the 18th president of the United States.

In 1979 Michael Jordan was cut from his high school basketball team. In 1998 he won his sixth NBA championship.

As a young man Walt Disney was fired from a newspaper due to "a lack of imagination."

Thomas Edison was told by one of his teachers that he was "too stupid to learn anything" and failed over 1,000 times before successfully inventing the light bulb.

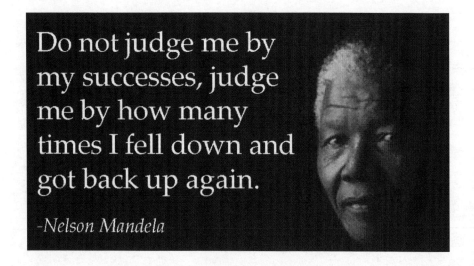

Do not judge me by my successes, judge me by how many times I fell down and got back up again.

-Nelson Mandela

"A GOOD MAN BRINGS GOOD THINGS OUT OF THE GOOD STORED UP IN HIS HEART, AND AN EVIL MAN BRINGS EVIL THINGS OUT OF THE EVIL STORED UP IN HIS HEART. FOR THE MOUTH SPEAKS WHAT THE HEART IS FULL OF. "

JESUS CHRIST - (LUKE 6:45)

"We need the iron qualities that go with true manhood. We need the positive virtues of resolution, of courage, of indomitable will, of power to do without shrinking the rough work that must always be done."

Theodore Roosevelt

"LIFE IS A STORM, MY YOUNG
FRIEND. YOU WILL BASK
IN THE SUNLIGHT ONE MO-
MENT, BE SHATTED ON THE
ROCKS THE NEXT. WHAT
MAKES YOU A MAN IS WHAT
YOU DO WHEN THAT STORM
COMES.

YOU MUST LOOK INTO THAT
STORM AND SHOUT AS YOU
DID IN ROME. DO YOUR
WORST, FOR I WILL DO
MINE!"

THE COUNT OF MONTE CRISTO

Nelson Mandela spent 27 years in a prison before being released and becoming the first black president of South Africa.

As a twelve year old boy actor Jim Carey was homeless. Now he is worth an estimated 150 million dollars.

Stephen King's first novel was rejected 30 times. Now his books have sold over 350 million copies and dozens have been made into movies.

Steven Spielberg, the most celebrated movie director of all time, was rejected by the University of Southern California's film school twice.

The common denominator in all these great men is grit.

Their hard work, courage and perseverance wouldn't allow their failures to become final.

Sir, I charge you to be a man of grit. A man who passionately pursues the plan that God has for you and refuses to quit no matter how many times you fail. Be a man not afraid to sweat to get where you're going.

Be passionate.

Be courageous.

Be tenacious.

Grab life by the horns, wrestle it to the ground, and refuse to give up until you breathe your last breath or it screams uncle. Be a man of grit.

Discussion Questions:

1. What does grit mean to you?

2. Who of the men above most inspire you to have grit? Why?

3. Do you think you have grit? Why? Or why not?

4. In what life situations could you prove your grit?

5. What have you quit in that past, that you will refuse to quit in the future?

A MAN TAKES RESPONSIBILITY FOR HIMSELF

A man takes responsibility for his actions and maintains self-control.

A man is responsible for himself. You will live in society where many, if not most people, want to blame everyone else for their shortcomings. They will blame the government, political leaders, the economy, their race, their parents, their spouse, their teachers, their bad luck, their god, the weather, their boss, the list could go on forever. But a real man chooses not to blame others. Instead he takes responsibility for his life. He understands that what you become tomorrow is simply the result of the decisions you make today. Therefore, while outside forces may play a role in a man's life, the real outcome is determined by his reactions, decisions and resolutions. Mark my words: In the long run, you almost always get what you deserve.

A real man chooses not to blame others. Instead he takes responsibility for his life.

President James A. Garfield was one of the poorest men to ever become president. The log cabin in rural Ohio where he was born was a far stretch from the White House in Washington. He was the youngest of five children and fatherless by the age of 2. Garfield certainly did not have the luxury of money to aid his early success. From an early age he worked as a carpenter and janitor. He paid his way through Williams College while working as a barge driver. Yet future President Garfield refused to allow his outside circumstances to dictate his future success. He never allowed his parents, his upbringing, or his lot in life to become an excuse for failure. Instead he took responsibility for himself. No one handed him success. In fact, what he was handed was hardship. But he eventually became president of the United States because he chose not to let life's circumstances keep him from his dreams.

Have you ever heard of Samuel Pierpont Langley? Probably not. In the early 1900's he was the man that everyone expected to build the first airplane. He was a mathematics professor at Harvard and a highly regarded senior officer at the Smithsonian Institute. He was friends with people like Alexander Graham Bell and Andrew Carnegie. He also had the money. The United States war department gave him $50,000, which was a fortune at the time, in order to fund the building of the first manned airplane. He had the brains, the money, the friends, the machinery... but you've never

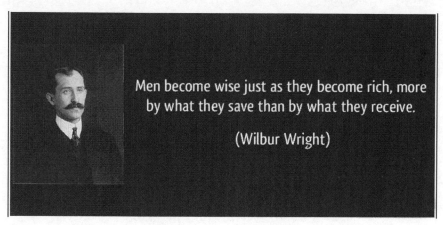

Men become wise just as they become rich, more by what they save than by what they receive.

(Wilbur Wright)

n. Why? Because a few hundred miles away in
ina, two brothers, Orville and Wilber Wright, who
the funding, clout or facilities given to Mr. Langley, began to creating the airplane. The Wright brothers
built the very first airplane in their bicycle shop without having
a single person on their team with an advanced degree.

Orville and Wilber Wright are famous because they refused to allow what they didn't have, to keep them from what they could have.

They took responsibility for their own success by do-
ing the best they could with what they had... and now they are
known around the world.

You will live in an era of "out of control" males. Road
rage, "flying off the handle" and "hot-headedness" will be
common when someone "disrespects" them. This is born of
irresponsibility and selfishness, and it's a counterfeit to true
manliness. You are not a man because you get mad and beat
someone up.

You are a man because you refuse to allow another person to determine how you react. Never say "they made me do
it." A real man is in control of himself - or said a different way
- a real man has self-control.

A real man has self-control.

"A man must at times be hard as nails: willing to face up to the truth about hi mself, and about the woman he loves, refusing compromise when compromise is wrong. But he must also be tender. No weapon will breach the armor of a woman's resentment like tenderness"
- Elisabeth Elliot

No one can "make" him do anything. He determines when to fight, when to speak, and when to raise his voice. And that decision should never be coerced by the actions of another person.

Sir, I charge you to be a man who takes responsibility for yourself. Never play "the blame game." Be responsible for your future no matter what life throws at you. Never let another
person control your actions.

Be a man of self-control.

You are your own captain.
Never relinquish leadership of your actions to any other mortal human.

Discussion Questions:

1. Have you easily made excuses in the past?

2. Why is it important not to make excuses and/or blame others?

3. When are you most tempted to make excuses and/or blame others?

4. Who is responsible for the man you become?

5. What steps can you take to start taking responsibility for your life?

A MAN HONORS OTHERS

A man has good friends because he is a good friend

Many males like to put others down. In order to build themselves up, they pick on, speak ill of and make fun of other men. While some of this can be done in playful fun and good jest, often it becomes a lifestyle of trying to win the battle of climbing the pecking order. This is not the way men were created to act.

A great man honors other men. He speaks good of them. Instead of finding their weakness and announcing it to the world, he compliments their strengths. A great man knows that everyone has weaknesses, embarrassing details and faults, but it is not his duty to amplify another man's shortcomings.

A man who honors other men will bring out the best in other men.

A man who honors other men will bring out the best in other men. He will not only be a great man, but he will also bring out the greatness in other men. He will always have plenty of friends, because men will want to be around him. And a man with many friends is a prosperous man.

Jackie Robinson was the first African American to play major league baseball. The racist jeering was relentless as many were not happy that baseball's "color barrier" had been breached. In his first seasons with the Brooklyn Dodgers he faced venom nearly everywhere he traveled. Fastballs were thrown at his head, he was intentionally stepped on with the

While playing a game in Cincinnati Ohio, Jackie committed an error. The fans began to ridicule him. It was the moment when it seemed as though the taunts and racial slurs had reached their peak. He stood at second base, humiliated, helpless, and dejected while the fans jeered. In the midst of Robinson's humiliation, Pee Wee Reese, a popular Southern white man who played shortstop, called timeout. He walked from his position at shortstop toward Robinson at second base, put his arm around Robinson's shoulder, and stood there with him for what seemed like a long time. The fans grew quiet.

The gesture spoke more eloquently than a thousand words. It said, this man is my friend.

Jackie Robinson later said that arm around his shoulder saved his career. Sometime later, when describing that moment, he explained, "Pee Wee kind of sensed the sort of helpless, dead feeling in me and came over and stood beside me for a while. He didn't say a word, but he looked over at the chaps who were yelling at me and just stared. He was standing by me, I could tell you that." (2)

Pee Wee Reese solidified his friendship with Jackie Robinson that day. Instead of joining in name calling, instead of complaining about his error in the play, he came to a friend's rescue with a gesture. He honored Jackie as a man, a baseball player and a friend. That's what a real man does.

A great man's love will be displayed by his action.

Sir, I charge you to be a man by honoring other men. Never allow negative words to flow from your mouth toward your friends. Speak life. Speak love. Speak words that honor. Be a good friend, and you will always have good friends.

"An acorn is not an oak when it is sprouted. It must go through long summers and fierce winters and endure all that frost, and snow, and thunder, and storms, and side-striking winds can bring, before it is a full grown oak. So a man is not a man when he is created; he is only begun. His manhood must come with years.

He who goes through life prosperous, and comes to his grace without a wrinkle, is not half a man. Difficulties are God's errands and trainers, and only through them can one come to fullness of manhood."

Henry Ward Beecher

Discussion Questions:

1. How do you think Jackie Robinson was feeling that day? Have you ever felt that way?

2. What do you think made Pee Wee Reese come to his side?

3. Do you use your words to honor other men or tear them down?

4. Describe what it looks like for men to honor each other.

5. What man do you need to honor today? Send him an honoring text now.

A MAN LOVES AND SERVES

A man loves and serves those under his care

As a man, you are expected to love. I know this may seem strange compared to the images of manhood in modern society that portray men as dominant and controlling, but you have a responsibility to love, protect and serve those under your supervision. That may be an employee, a student, a soldier, a child at church, your wife, or your own children. God has given each man the responsibility to lovingly care for those under his umbrella of leadership. A great man will take this responsibility seriously. He will put himself in harm's way to protect others. He will go without so that others can have. A great man's love will be displayed by his action.

It was a hot July day during the American Revolution. A group of weary soldiers were repairing a small defensive barrier when a man in civilian clothes rode past. Their leader, a pompous young corporal, was shouting instructions to his men, but making no attempt to help them. When the rider noticed the exasperated soldiers being harassed by their leader, he asked the Corporal why he was shouting and not helping. The man retorted with great dignity, "Sir, I am a corporal!" The stranger apologized, dismounted, and then began to help the exhausted soldiers. When the job was done, he turned to the corporal and said, "Mr. Corporal, next time you have a job like this and not enough men to do it, go to your commander-in-chief, and I will come and help you again." The man was dumbfounded, for this had been none other than General George Washington.

"I HOPE I SHALL POSSESS FIRMNESS AND VIRTURE ENOUGH TO MAINTAIN WHAT I CONSIDER THE MOST ENVIABLE OF ALL TITLES, THE CHARACTER OF AN HONEST MAN."

GEORGE WASHINGTON

It is impossible to reightly govern a nation without God and the Bible"
-George Washington

George Washington was known as a man who loved, protected and served those who were under his leadership. In August 1776, General George Washington found himself and his army in the midst of a life threatening situation. The British outnumbered the Continental Army almost four to one, and the Americans were low on gun powder and supplies. To lead his troops into battle would certainly mean defeat, and to surrender was out of the question.

Adversity is the testing ground of the character and resolve of a man.

As fear spread throughout the Continental Camp a young lieutenant asked "What are we going to do?" General George Washington replied, "Firmly rely on the protection of Divine Providence. God has not brought us this far to desert us." The Americans braced themselves and awaited the British attack throughout the day, but it never came. It was that evening when George Washington came up with a dar-

"*Masculinity is not something given to you, but something you gain. And you gain it by winning small battles with honor.*"
Normal Mailer

ing - almost crazy - plan of escape. By night, he would se-
cretly evacuate the entire army (8,000 men) across the East
River. This seemed preposterous because the river was at
least a mile wide. The British would certainly see the boats
and men in the moonlight, or hear their oars hitting the
water, not to mention the sound of 8,000 moving men - no
matter how quiet they might try to be. How could this plan
possibly succeed?

All night long the Americans gathered in row boats
making the dangerous two mile roundtrip voyage to one
side and back. They moved soldiers, canons, supplies,

*Washington, in an incredible example of love for
his men, refused to leave for safety while he still
had men in harm's way.*

and even cattle and horses. Miraculously the dark of night
had concealed their escape, but as daylight broke they were
far from complete.

They needed at least three more hours to finish and
would certainly be spotted in the daylight. Washington, in
an incredible example of love for his men, refused to leave
for safety while he still had men in harm's way. He was ada-
mant that he would be the last man brought to safety.

It was in this moment that the providence of God
showed up. Unexpectedly, a dense fog rose onto the river
and covered both military encampments making it impossible for them to see one another. It was reported that men
had less than twenty feet of visibility. In what can only be
explained as a miracle, the fog remained until the last boat

– the one carrying General George Washington - had left the shore.

As the fog lifted and the British were shocked to find the American encampment empty. They began firing at the last few boats, but they were now well out of range for the British muskets.

George Washington loved, served and protected his soldiers. He created the plan, and then left himself to be the last one removed from danger. This is what a man does. He loves, serves and protects those under his care. He prays for them and leads them with their best interest in mind.

Gentlemen, I charge you love and serve those in which the Lord gives you authority.

Discussion Questions:

1. What areas are you involved in leadership?

2. What does servant leadership mean to you?

3. What would it look like for you to lead through love?

4. Do you know who leads through love? Do you know someone who leads through dominance and tyranny? Who would you rather follow?

5. What is one step you can begin taking this week to be a more loving, protecting and serving leader?

A MAN HAS INTEGRITY

A man doesn't make decisions based on consequences

You live in a world vastly devoid of character and integrity. These are the qualities that make you the same when people are looking... and when they're not. Integrity is what you do when "that" movie comes on TV and no one is home. C.S. Lewis once said "Surely what a man does when he is taken off his guard is the best evidence for what sort of man he is. If there are rats in a cellar, you are most likely to see them if you go in very suddenly. But the suddenness does not create the rats; it only prevents them from hiding. In the same way, the suddenness of the provocation does not make me ill-tempered; it only shows me what an ill-tempered man I am." Integrity is proven in your choices during hard times.

Too many males make decisions based on consequences. Whether they cheat on a test, cheat on their wife, or take something that doesn't belong to them, their actions are not determined by what's right, but by the likelihood of getting caught. Whether they stand for truth is determined by what others will say or think. Real men make decisions based on what's right and wrong, not the consequences that might come from their decisions.

The World War II generation has been called the greatest generation to ever live. The men of WWII were a different breed. Many sought to get to the front of draft line. They were eager to fight Hitler, the Germans and the Japanese. My best friend from childhood was Joey. His grandfather ate ten

They knew they may return wounded, in wheelchairs, or not at all. Yet they kissed loved ones goodbye and enthusiastically enlisted to fight.

pounds of bananas to make the military's weight requirement so he could enlist! These men were intent on fighting the evils of Nazi Germany despite the consequences. They knew they may return wounded, in wheelchairs, or not at all. Yet they kissed loved ones goodbye and enthusiastically enlisted to

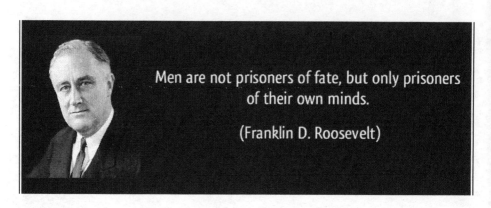

Men are not prisoners of fate, but only prisoners of their own minds.

(Franklin D. Roosevelt)

fight. They did what was right, no matter the consequences. On June 6th 1944, 150,000 brave men stormed the 50 miles of beaches in Normandy, France. This attack became known as D-day, and was the largest amphibious attack in history. Nearly 4,000 troops died on the beach.

Later that day, President Franklin D. Roosevelt led the nation in prayer saying

Almighty God: our sons, pride of our Nation, this day have set upon a   mighty endeavor, a struggle to preserve our Republic, our religion, and our civilization, and to set free a suffering humanity. Lead them straight and true; give strength to their arms, stoutness to their hearts, stead-fastness in their faith... They will be sore tired, by night and by day, without rest - until the victory is won. The darkness will be rent by noise and flame. Men's souls will be shaken with the violences of war... With Thy blessings, we shall prevail over the unholy forces of our enemy. Help us to conquer the apostles of greed and racial arrogancies. Lead us to the saving of our country (3)

Ten weeks after D-day, all of Northern France had been liberated from German control. This paved the way for American advances throughout Europe and eventually winning the war. President Roosevelt and our American soldiers chose to do what was right, no matter the **Integrity is proven in your choices during hard times.** consequences. They fought, bled, went hungry, thirsty, were wounded and many lost their lives for the cause of justice. They believed they were fighting for what was right, and most returned with more scars than metals or recognition.

They are the greatest generation because they did what was right despite the consequences.

Integrity is what you do when "that" movie comes on TV and no one is home.

Pastor Chuck Swindoll once wrote:

THE WORLD NEEDS MEN...who cannot be bought; whose word is their bond; who put character above wealth; who possess opinions and a will; who are larger than their vocations; who do not hesitate to take chances; who will not lose their individuality in a crowd; who will be as honest in small things as in great things; who will make no compromise with wrong; whose ambitions are not confined to their own selfish desires; who will not say they do it " because everybody else does it"; who are true to their friends through good report and evil report, in adversity as well as in prosperity; who do not believe that shrewdness, cunning, and hardheadedness are the best qualities for winning success; who are not ashamed or afraid to stand for the truth when it is unpopular; who can say "no" with emphasis, a though all the rest of the world says "yes." (4)

Sir, I charge you to be a man of integrity. I charge you to make decisions based on what's right, not what's easy. I charge you to stand for truth... come what may.

Discussion Questions:

1. What is your definition of integrity?

2. Why do you think that so few men have genuine integrity?

3. Do you ever make moral decisions based on the consequences of your decisions?

4. When is the last time you had a hard time making a moral decision? Why?

5. Is it more important to be right before God, or be popular before man?

A MAN CONFRONTS EVIL

A man confronts evil, pursues justice and loves mercy

As you have seen throughout this book, being a man is in no regard an easy undertaking. A man must know when to speak and when to be silent. When confronted with evil, a great man will always stand up against it. As the 18th century statesman Edmund Burke once said, "The only thing necessary for the triumph of evil is for good men to do nothing." When faced with the adversity of evil, great men refuse to shrink back. Instead, they rise up no matter the odds with a spirit that pursues justice.

Abraham Lincoln was elected to be the 16th president of the United States in 1860. Realizing the challenges that lie ahead, he openly opposed the practice of slavery. It would have certainly been easier to remain silent before the sin of slavery, but great men answer the deep inner call to confront evil. Lincoln could not ignore evil. It had to be confronted. Justice had to be pursued for all. This opposition to slavery led seven southern states to form the Confederate States of America before he even moved into the White House. Yet Lincoln refused to compromise regarding slavery. It was an evil that must be confronted. He once said "slavery is founded on the selfishness of man's nature; opposition to it on his love of justice." [5]

When faced with the adversity of evil, great men refuse to shrink back. Instead, they rise up no matter the odds with a spirit that pursues justice.

"I do order and declare that all persons held as **Slaves** within said designated States, and parts of States, **Are** and henceforward shall be **Free.**

- President Lincoln, 22 September 1862

President Lincoln's stance against slavery led to the bloodiest war in US history. Approximately 620,000 soldiers died from combat, starvation, or disease during the Civil War. That's more than 200,000 more than any other war. Yet he did not hold back, compromise or whither during in his fight against injustice. Even in the early years when the union was losing nearly every battle, he stood resolute.

In March of 1863, as General Robert E. Lee marched toward Washington DC, President Lincoln issued a proclamation calling for a day of fasting. He knew that if the confederates reached Washington, his cause was almost certainly lost. In that address he stated,

We have been the recipients of the choicest bounties of Heaven. We have been preserved, these many years, in peace and prosperity. We have grown in numbers, wealth and power, as no other nation has ever grown. But we have forgotten God. We have forgotten the gracious hand which preserved us in peace, and multiplied and enriched and strengthened us; and we have vainly imagined, in the deceitfulness of our hearts, that all these blessings were produced by some superior wisdom and virtue of our own. Intoxicated with unbroken success, we have become too self-sufficient to feel the necessity of redeeming and preserving grace, too proud to pray to the God that made us!

It behooves us then, to humble ourselves before the offended Power, to confess our national sins, and to pray for clemency and forgiveness.

Now, therefore, in compliance with the request, and fully concurring in the views of the Senate, I do, by this my proclamation, designate and set apart Thursday, the 30th. day of April, 1863, as a day of national humiliation, fasting and prayer. And I do hereby request all the People to abstain, on that   day, from their ordinary secular pursuits, and to unite, at their several places of public worship and their respective homes, in keeping the day holy to the Lord, and devoted to the humble discharge of the religious duties proper to that solemn occasion.

All this being done, in sincerity and truth, let us then rest humbly in the hope authorized by the Divine teachings, that the united cry of the Nation will be heard on high, and answered with blessings, no less than the pardon of our national sins, and the restoration of our now divided and suffering Country, to its former happy condition of unity and peace. (6)

As General Lee led the southern army into Gettysburg Pennsylvania, they were marching headstrong toward Washington. Lincoln knew this battle would be pivotal for the outcome of the war. So while the battle of Gettysburg raged, he went to his room, locked the door, and knelt down before Almighty God. He prayed with the fervor and passion of a man determined to win victory against evil. In his own words he later said, "I told him that this was His war, and our cause was His cause, but we couldn't stand another Fredericksburg or Chancellorsville. And I then and there made a solemn vow to Almighty God, that if He would stand with you boys at Gettysburg I would stand with Him." (7)

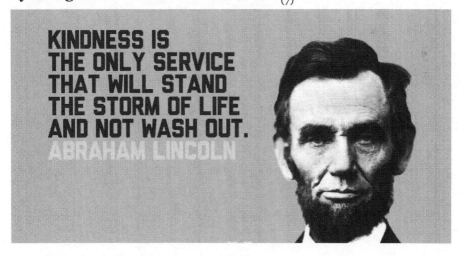

KINDNESS IS THE ONLY SERVICE THAT WILL STAND THE STORM OF LIFE AND NOT WASH OUT.
ABRAHAM LINCOLN

For the first time in a strategic battle, the Union won convincing over the Confederates at Gettysburg. Three days of intense fighting had culminated in an estimated 51,000 casualties that ended with General Lee's army retreating back to Virginia. Gettysburg became the turning point of the war. From that point on the Union army began to win the war. Finally on April 9, 1865 the Civil War officially ended when Robert E. Lee surrendered the last major Confederate army at the Appomattox Courthouse in Virginia.

President Lincoln's pursuit of justice led to his leading the charge to confront evil. It was a long and difficult charge full of arduous decisions that led to many deaths and much blood. For all those wanting to be men, this is your duty as well. You must confront evil... Being a man means taking a stand against the evils of this world - and at times it means waging war against the evil you may find within yourself.

Gentlemen, I charge you to learn from the example of President Abraham Lincoln and confront evil and pursue justice... It will never be easy. But it is what a great man does.

Discussion Questions:

1. What opportunities do you have to confront evil?

2. What does pursuing justice mean to you?

3. What might prevent you from confronting evil?

4. Is there a time in the past that you have confronted evil?

5. Is there something that makes you think "someone should do something about this!"? Perhaps that someone is you. What steps can you begin taking to rectify this evil?

A MAN HONORS GOD

A man loves the Lord with all his heart, soul and mind

The ultimate source of strength in a great man is not found in his muscles, his resolve, or his intellect. It cannot be enhanced by protein shakes, or taken by age. A great man's strength comes from The Lord. King David's exploits make him arguably the most courageous man in the entire Bible. He said "The LORD is my strength and my shield; my heart trusts in him, and he helps me." (Psalm 28:7) Some have falsely assumed that prayer is a sign of weakness, but that is not true. A great man knows that his strength is found in the place of prayer. Great men study their Bible and have a deep relationship with Jesus Christ. They strive to live a life surrendered to The One who has authority to empower their lives. They live holy from the inside out.

Many of the influential men of history knew our Great God. Most of the greatest philosophers, scientists and thinkers knew God. Of the great men who founded our nation, the vast majority relied on Christ for their wisdom, strength and abilities. He was their help, just as He will be your help.

A great man's strength comes from The Lord.

Founding Father John Adams said "The Christian religion is, above all the religions that ever prevailed or existed in ancient or modern times, the religion of wisdom, virtue, equity and humanity." (8)

60

The courage we desire and prize is not the courage to die decently, but to live manfully.
Thomas Carlyle

> "WASTE NO MORE TIME ARGUING WHAT A GOOD MAN SHOULD BE. *BE ONE.*"
>
> MARCUS AURELIUS

Signer of the Declaration of Independence, Samuel Adams, said "The name of the Lord (says the Scripture) is a strong tower; thither the righteous flee and are safe [Proverbs 18:10].

Let us secure His favor and He will lead us through the journey of this life and at length receive us to a better." [9] Revolutionary General Patrick Henry said "Being a Christian... is a character which I prize far above all this world has or can boast." [10]

The original chief Justice of the Supreme Court, John Jay, said "The Bible is the best of all books, for it is the word of God and teaches us the way to be happy in this world and in the next. Continue therefore to read it and to regulate your life by its precepts." [11]

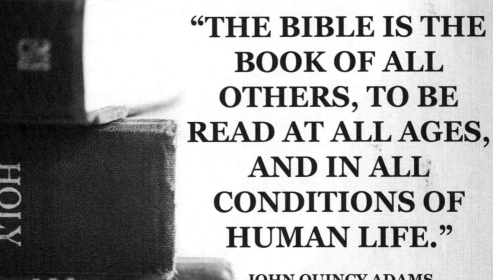

"THE BIBLE IS THE BOOK OF ALL OTHERS, TO BE READ AT ALL AGES, AND IN ALL CONDITIONS OF HUMAN LIFE."

JOHN QUINCY ADAMS

"When I was a child, I talked like a child, I thought like a child, I reasoned like a child. When I become a man, I put the ways of childhood behind me."
1 Corinthians 13:11

Father of the public school system, and signer of the Declaration of Independence Benjamin Rush said "The Bible contains more knowledge necessary to man in his present state than any other book in the world." [12]

James A. Garfield was our 20th president. He was a preacher who once preached 19 times during a revival saying he had 34 people come to Christ - and he baptized 31 of them! His strength was found in The Lord.

John Quincy Adams was the sixth president of the United States and probably the most intelligent president. He spoke and wrote seven languages by age 10! He was a devout Christian who found his strength in prayer and study of the Bible. In 1811, while serving as an ambassador in St Petersburg, Russia, he wrote a letter to his son stating:

"I advise you, my son, in whatever you read, and most of all in reading the Bible, to remember that it is for the purpose of making you wiser and more virtuous. I have myself, for many years, made it a practice to read through the Bible once every year... in your infancy and youth, you have been, and will be for some years under the authority and control of your friends and instructors; but you must soon come to the age where you must govern yourself. You have already come to that age in many respects; you know the difference between right and wrong, and you know some of the duties, and the obligations you are under, to become acquainted to them all. It is in the Bible, you must learn them, and from the Bible how to practice them. Those duties are to God, to your fellow creatures, and to yourself." [13]

Graffiti from the 1800s discovered by workers renovating the Washington Monument has quite a different tone from that usually found today on the sides of buildings and subway cars. It reads, "Whoever is the human instrument under God in the conversion of one soul, erects a monument to his own memory more lofty and enduing than this." (14) This inscription can now be viewed by visitors to the monument. It is signed BFB. No one knows who that is, but I'm confident he was a real man...

Great men know their strength comes from The Lord. You live in a humanistic society where man is exalted and people are taught that they have all they need within themselves.

Gentlemen, I charge you to find your strength in Jesus. Honor the Lord in all you do. Live fully surrendered to him - because great men always do.

Discussion Questions

1. When is the last time you spent time talking to the Lord?

2. In what ways does the Lord give you strength?

3. Name 5 of the greatest men in history. Who did these men call their God?

4. What prevents you from putting your trust in Jesus?

5. What steps can you take to begin seeking the Lord's strength?

A MAN STANDS FOR TRUTH

A man who doesn't stand for truth will fall for anything

You live in a world full of political correctness and an almost constant fear of offending someone. The fear of offending people has led many to abandon truth - since truth is by its very nature always exclusive and offensive.

A real man stands for truth. While he is never purposely offensive or hurtful, he understands that truth is necessary to honor both God and the world. Political correctness is always ultimately more hurtful than standing for truth in the first place. Like stretching back a rubber band, it simply prolongs and increases the inevitable blunt force of the truth.

All truth is ultimately found in The Lord.

The world is daily becoming more pluralistic and relativistic. Therefore, it is more important than ever that men take a stand for truth.

Standing up for truth will be no easy task. There will be many dissenters and haters. But the same person from whom truth comes from is the same person who will give you the strength to stand for that truth. The Reverend Doctor Martin Luther King Jr knew this well. He stood up against incredible opposition as he proclaimed the Biblical truth that all men were created equal. He was stabbed, beaten and imprisoned numerous times for his stance on truth. Yet he never wavered. He stood absolute on his convictions and it gave resolve to all those who followed him. How was he able to stand for truth amidst such persecution? How could he find the strength to move forward knowing his wife and daughter were also at risk? Well, the Reverend King once explained his resolve in a sermon he preached...

I sat at the table thinking about my daughter and thinking about the fact that she could be taken away from me any minute. And I started thinking about a dedicated, devoted and loyal wife, she was over there asleep.... And I got to the point that I couldn't take it anymore. I was weak...

And I discovered that religion had to become real to me, and I had to know God for myself. And I bowed over the cup of coffee. I never will forget it... I prayed a prayer, and I prayed out loud that night. I said, "Lord, I'm down here trying to do what's right. I think it's right. I think the cause that we represent is right. But, Lord, I must confess that I'm weak now. I'm a faltering. I'm losing my courage..."

And it seemed at that moment that I could hear an inner voice saying to me, "Martin Luther stand up for righteousness. Stand up for justice. Stand up for truth. And I will be with you, even until the end of the world..." I heard

I have a dream that my four little children will one day live in a nation where they will not be judged by the color of their skin, but by the content of their character.

~ Martin Luther King

God was with Dr. King. He faced many more trials and many more difficulties. And on August 28, 1963, he gave an impromptu speech that still rings across America. More than 250,000 people had marched into Washington DC for a rally urging congress to pass civil rights legislation. The rally was being held on the steps of the Lincoln memorial. As Reverend King was about to sit down, gospel singer Mahalia Jackson yelled out, "Tell them about your dream, Martin! Tell them about your dream!" He then proceeded to deliver one of the most extraordinary speeches in American history. This is when he said these iconic words....

"I have a dream that one day this nation will rise up and live out the true meaning of its creed: 'We hold these truths to be self-evident, that all men are created equal.' I have a dream that one day on the red hills of Georgia, the sons of former slaves and the sons of former slave owners will be able to sit down together at the table of brotherhood. I have a dream that one day even the state of Mississippi, a state sweltering with the heat of injustice, sweltering with the heat of oppression, will be transformed into an oasis of freedom and justice. I have a dream that my four little children will one day live in a nation where they will not be judged by the color of their skin but by the content of their character. I have a dream today!" (16)

Rev Martin Luther King Jr stood for truth - God's truth - in the midst of opposition and hardship, eventually giving his life for this cause. This truth came from the Bible and his empowerment to stand for it came from his relationship with Jesus Christ.

Gentlemen, of all the challenges I give you in this book, this may be the most difficult. I understand that standing for truth might mean you'll be called names, persecuted, ostracized and possibly even put in jail during your lifetime. But I charge you to stand for truth and lean on the Lord for your strength. Do not be wishy washy or lukewarm.

For the man who stands for truth on earth will be able to stand before God in heaven.

Discussion Questions:

1. What is truth?

2. Why is standing for truth so hard?

3. Have you ever failed to stand for truth? Explain.

4. What would it look like for you to stand for truth in the environment of your world (school, work, etc.)?

5. Imagine a situation where you will stand for truth and play out the scenario in your mind.

A MAN PROTECTS

A man helps those who are weaker

A man protects those who are weaker. He doesn't bully others. Instead, a great man stands up against bullies. A man understands that God has given him strengths, not for his own glory, but for the purpose of assisting those who are weaker. Men with strong muscles help and protect those who are weaker. Men who have supreme intelligence should use it to help those who struggle to learn. Men who have more finances should help those in need.

All God's gifts are given for the purpose of benefiting and helping others.

When men stop protecting the weaker, a hierarchical bullying system begins to occur. These tyrants will use their strength to lord over and oppress others. This is precisely what began to occur when the Nazi regime came to power in 1933. Because of their deeply held theories, which were rooted in Darwinian Evolution, the Nazis believed that they were superior humans. They slowly and methodically began spewing propaganda attempting to demonize Jews. When good men did not speak out against this propaganda, it eventually grew to the systematic killing of people with disabilities. At least 200,000 physically or mentally disabled patients were murdered by the Nazis. When men did not stand up to pro-

ect these weaker vessels, the Nazi's moved on to persecut-
ng Jewish people and other races they deemed less worthy.
At first they were publically humiliated, placed into ghettos
and shamed by society. Eventually these people were moved
o death camps where they would be worked unceasingly,
experimented on, and tortured.

As strong men continued to do nothing, the weak
were kept in the worst possible conditions. Starved and
naked, many froze to death, died of common sicknesses
or died of starvation. The ones who were not even deemed
worthy of being placed in death camps were systematically
killed in gas chambers. In all, nearly eleven million people
were executed during the Nazi regime.

*Eleven million lives were exterminaed because
men did not stand up against bullies named
Adolf Hitler and Joseph Stalin.*

There was at least one man who helped protect the Jews. His name was Oskar Schindler. He risked his life to hide Jews as workers in his ammunitions factory, and gave nearly all his fortune toward bribing Nazi soldiers with large gifts and money to look the other way. Against the hideously dark backdrop of the Nazi regime, Oskar Schindler stood out like a shining star. He is credited with saving at least 1,200 Jewish men and women from execution.

Schindler gave of his finances, influence and business to help the Jews during their time of stress. He was a real man. He once said, "I had to help them. I had no choice."(17) He used what The Lord had given him to help those in need and rescue them from their oppressors. Strong men must stand up to tyrants.

Sir, I charge you to be a man who protects those who are weaker than you.

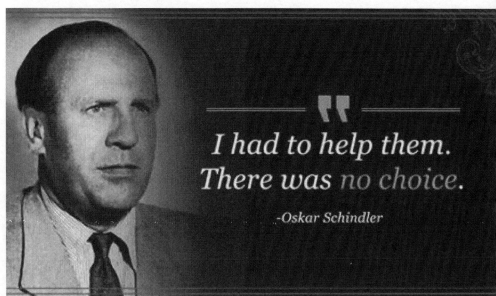

I had to help them. There was no choice.

-Oskar Schindler

Discussion Questions:

1. Why do you think the common people allowed the mistreatment of the Jews?

2. Have you seen people take advantage of the weaker? How have you responded?

3. Why did you respond that way?

4. In what ways have you been blessed with strength? (Physical, Mental, Emotional, Intellectual, Spiritual, Health, Financial)

5. How can you use your strength to help the weak?

A MAN IS A PROPHET

A man has power to call greatness out of people

A man's mouth is a powerful weapon. Proverbs 18:21 says, "Death and life are in the power of the tongue." All the way back in the garden of Eden God gave Adam the authority to name the animals. The prophetic ability to both see and speak to the diamond in the rough is a great responsibility that few men understand. Many sons and daughters will rise or fall based on what a father speaks over them. Many wives will emotionally live or die based on what a husband speaks over her. Companies, cities, churches and colleges are all affected by the prophetic voice of the man.

When a man understands this gift, it is a beautiful thing. Just as a small acorn can become a mighty oak tree, so the man is gifted to look into others and see gifts, talents and abilities that are seeds of greatness. A man's prophetic words become the water that inspires seeds of greatness to grow. That's why a man must always speak life and good of others - especially those under his spiritual and/or leadership "covering" (wife, children, employees, etc.). He's been given the ability to build them up for greatness, or tear them down to destruction with his words. Prophetic words speak to what people are called to, not necessarily what they are.

A man's prophetic words become the water that inspires seeds of greatness to grow.

A man's words were made to inspire greatness. That's why motivational speakers are paid hundreds of thousands of dollars to speak for 40 minutes at a banquet. Your words were made to motivate. That's why coaches make pregame speeches, politicians make nomination speeches, valedictorians make class speeches, and pastors preach sermons. It's because our words have the ability to inspire people to go farther, reach deeper and fight harder. Words are more powerful than most men realize.

Remember when William Wallace needed to inspire his countrymen? He said "fight and you may die. Run and you'll live -- at least a while. And dying in your beds many years from now, would you be willing to trade all the days from this day to that for one chance, just one chance to come back here and tell our enemies that they may take our lives, but they'll never take our freedom!!!" Doesn't it just make you want to pick up a sword and kilt and run into battle beside Wallace!

How about when Rocky Balboa needed to motivate his son and said:

"I'd hold you up to say to your mother, 'this kid's gonna be the best kid in the world. This kid's gonna be somebody better than anybody I ever knew.' And you grew up good and wonderful. It was great just watching you, every day was like a privilege. Then the time came for you to be your own man and take on the world, and you did. But somewhere along the line, you changed. You stopped being you. You let people stick a finger in your face and tell you you're no good. And when things got hard, you started looking for something to blame, like a big shadow. Let me tell you something you already know. The world ain't all sunshine and rainbows. It's a very mean and nasty place and I don't care how tough you are it will beat you to your knees and keep you there permanently if you let it. You, me, or nobody is gonna hit as hard as life. But it ain't about how hard you hit. It's about how hard you can get hit and keep moving forward. How much you can take and keep moving forward. That's how winning is done! Now if you know what you're worth then go out and get what you're worth. But ya gotta be willing to take the hits, and not pointing fingers saying you ain't where you wanna be because of him, or her, or anybody! Cowards do that and that ain't you! You're better than that! I'm always gonna love you no matter what. No matter what happens. You're my son and you're my blood. You're the best thing in my life. But until you start believing in yourself, ya ain't gonna have a life."

"Adversity toughens manhood, and the characteristic of the good or the great man is not that he has been exempt from the evils of life, but that he has surmounted them."

Patrick Henry

"YOU SEEK THE HEIGHTS OF MANHOOD WHEN YOU SEEK THE DEPTHS OF GOD."

EDWIN LOUIS COLE

I want to be a better man after that speech! Why? Because words were made to prophetically inspire us to want to be great.

All men fail. What makes them great men is that when they fail they get back up, brush themselves off and start again.

Gentlemen, your mouth is a powerful prophetic weapon - for good or evil. I charge you to use it wisely. Speak to people in such a way that inspires greatness. Name people according to their potential, not their current failings.

Speak over people the same words that your Heavenly Father is speaking over them.

Be a powerful prophetic voice.

Discussion Questions:

1. What makes a man's words so powerful?

2. Do you ever tear people down with your words?

3. How do you feel when people you respect speak good
things
about you?

4. Do you want to be known as a person who encourages or
discourages others?

5. Name three people you will begin purposely speaking good
words toward this week.

CONCLUSION

In conclusion, there's a few more thing I want you to know.

First of all, I realize the principles in this book may be intimidating. You need to know that there's not a man alive who has fulfilled the tenets of this manifesto perfectly. All men fail. What makes them great men is that when they fail they get back up, brush themselves off and start again. They fail forward. In other words, they learn from their failures. Never allow your failures as a man to be the final word. Proverbs 24:16 says "The godly may trip seven times, but they will get up again. But one disaster is enough to overthrow the wicked."

Your success as a man is not dependent on being perfect - No man is perfect. Your success as a man is determined by your striving to become a better man each day, week, month and year that you live. Becoming a great man is a process. It's a lifelong progression of failing forward. It's consistently... Growing. Developing. Learning. Gaining wisdom. Getting better. That's what becoming a man means. Second, you can only be a great man to the extent that you're surrendered to Jesus Christ. True greatness will never be found outside of Him. I know you may be tempted to pass this by. But if the Lord tarries, there will be times in your life when you need to be reminded that making Jesus the Lord of your life is the key to greatness. Never forget that.

Now, go discover the great man that lies within you.

Brent

THE MAN'S MANIFESTO

Gentlemen, as you strive to become the man
that God has called you to be, I charge you to:

Work hard and never quit amidst opposition.

Take responsibility for your actions and maintain self-control.

Honor others by being a good friend.

Love and serve those under your care.

Never make decisions based on consequences.

Confront evil, pursue justice and love mercy.

Love the Lord your God with all your heart, soul and mind.

Stand for truth.

Help those who are weaker.

Speak prophetically over people.

I accept this charge.

Name: _____

Date: _____

A MESSAGE TO FATHERS

Hey Dads!

This book was originally written for my son on his 13th birth-day. It was the culmination of a weeklong "Becoming a Man" trip we made together in Washington D.C.

Each of the stories in this book were meant to coincide with a specific location (often a monument) in Washington D.C. or the surrounding area. At each of these locations I told my son the stories that are written in this book. I then charged him to be a man in accordance with the topic addressed - The same charges that are given throughout this book. Then I sealed it with a prayer over him that was specific to the charge. This was a powerful experience for both my son and I.

The original document also held a "father's blessing" that I had written to my son. People often ask how I decided what to say for my sons blessing. It was relatively simple. I prayed and asked the Lord what was inside my son that I needed to call forth. Then I began writing down the things that came to came to my mind and corresponded with the potential I could see in him.

I plan to do these trips twice with my sons (and Lord willing grandsons). Once at age 13 and again at age 18. And I plan to give them a father's blessing at the end of each. The "Becoming a Man" trip comes at age 13. The other (yet unnamed) trip comes at age 18.

I only share this because I believe your sons are longing to be taught what it means to be great men. Whether you go on a trip to D.C., an outdoor camping journey, or just have consistent strategic conversations, I charge you to intentionally teach your kids about manhood. If you don't teach them, their friends and the television will - and they will join multitudes of males who have never learned to be men. So spend time planning it. Organize your thoughts, and intentionally teach your boys the art of manliness.

If I can be of assistance in this process, please don't hesitate to contact me. You can email me at pastorbrent@brandonag.org

Brent Simpson has been in ministry since 1998 and is currently the senior pastor of Brandon Assembly of God in Brandon Florida. Brandon Assembly is a rapidly growing and vibrant church that strives to create an atmosphere where God moves. He also currently serves as the Presbyter for Section 10 of the Pen Florida District of the Assemblies of God.

Brent has ministered as a youth pastor, music pastor, senior pastor, evangelist, apologist, teacher and musician. He has been a key speaker at conferences, conventions, rallies, revivals and the like. He has ministered in more than thirty countries. He is the author of Where's the Beef? Reclaiming the Power of God in your Life and Ministry, Your Life is an

Epic Story, the TRUTH apologetics curriculum and several other DVD based small group curriculum and materials

Pastor Brent & his wife Ada are passionate about leading people to Jesus, and consistently see healings, deliverance and other miraculous signs in their meetings.

Brent is a graduate of Trinity College where he was trained in the area of theology and apologetics, and is currently earning a Master's Degree in Ministerial Leadership from Southeastern University. Brent has three amazing children, and has been married to his beautiful wife Ada since 2000.

For more information visit www.brentsimpson.com

NOTES

1. Donald J. Palmisano, On Leadership: Essential Principles for Business, Political, and Personal Success (New York, Skyhorse, 2011), 50.
2. http://www.nytimes.com/2005/11/02/sports/baseball/two-men-who-did-the-right-thing.html?_r=0
3. http://www.historyplace.com/speeches/fdr-prayer.htm
4. Charles Swindoll, Living Above the Level of Mediocrity: A commitment to Excellence (Nashville, Thomas Nelson, 1989)107-8.
5. http://www.abrahamlincolnonline.org/lincoln/speeches/slavery.htm
6. http://www.abrahamlincolnonline.org/lincoln/speeches/fast.htm
7. Robert R. Mathisen, The Routledge Source of Religion and the Civil War: A History in Documents (New York, Routledge, 2015), 280.
8. http://www.thefederalistpapers.org/founders/john-adams
9. Barak Josiah, The United States, Law, Government, Religion, Christianity, and Illegalities (Bloomington, Westbow, 2011) 217.
10. Ibid, 219.
11. James H. Hutson, The Founders on Religion: A Book of Quotations (New Jersey, Princeton, 2005) 52.
12. Charles D. Cleveland, A Compendium of American Literature (Philadelphia, Biddle, 1858) 82.
13. http://providencefoundation.com/?page_id=2536
14. http://www.nytimes.com/1994/07/17/us/theological-graffiti-found-in-monument.html
15. Philip Yancey, Soul Survivor: How My Faith Survived the Church (New York, Doubleday, 2001) 86.
16. Gary Laderman, and Luis Leon, Religion and American Cultures: An Encyclopedia of Traditions, Diversity and Popular Expressions (Santa Barbara, ABC Clio, 2003) 866.
17. http://www.oskarschindler.dk/schindler9.htm

58807219R10057

Made in the USA
Charleston, SC
21 July 2016